·AMAZING·
DOG TRICKS

Cover and interior images: Shutterstock.com

Contributing writer: Donald Vaughan

Louis Weber, CEO
Publications International, Ltd.
8140 Lehigh Avenue
Morton Grove, Illinois 60053

Permission is never granted for commercial purposes.

ISBN: 978-1-68022-585-3

Manufactured in China

8 7 6 5 4 3 2 1

Table of Contents

Introduction

So your dog knows how to sit, stay, and lie down...but what else can the two of you do? In this book, we'll explore a number of fun tricks you and your dog can learn. Some, like fetching, can be useful. Others, like dancing, can help your dog stay active. Still others are just cute tricks that will impress your friends!

Most tricks are taught via the clicker training method. The clicker is a way to implement positive reinforcement. When the dog does something right, you click. After clicking, reward your dog with a treat or praise, so that the dog knows that clicking indicates that he's done well. (Why click instead of just praising or treating? Because clicking is a single, consistent sound that's easy for the dog to learn and associate with a specific action on his part.)

As you train, always make sure to click exactly as a behavior is being performed, not before or after. If you click too early or too late, you may end up reinforcing the wrong behavior—for example, if your dog raises her paw to shake hands but then drops it, you want to make sure to click before she drops her paw. Otherwise you end up rewarding her putting her paw down instead of raising it.

If you haven't used clicker training before, you'll want to "charge" the clicker before beginning to teach any of the tricks in this book. To do this, you want to set up the association in your dog's mind between clicks and treats. So when you and your dog are together, click, then treat. Do this many times so that your dog begins to look forward to hearing the sound. Then move to just treating if your dog responds to the click by paying attention.

When you train, you'll be clicking and treating at several stages, not just when the final trick is performed. Generally each trick is built of many small steps, and you'll want to click and treat each step as you build the behavior.

Are you ready? I'm ready!

CLICKER Training Tips

Here are some tips to get the most out of your training sessions:

🐾 Keep your sessions short. Don't train if your dog is tired or frustrated—you want your pooch to think training time is fun and exciting, a special time.

Of course I'm proud of my film work, but my real dream is to direct.

SCENE	CUT	TAKE
DATE		ROLL
PROD.CO.		
DIRECTOR		CAMERAMAN

🐾 Break down each desired behavior into small steps. If your dog doesn't seem to be getting some part of the trick, try to see if you can't break the step down into smaller sub-steps. Click and treat at each small step.

🐾 Always reward your dog for doing well. You don't need to always give food treats, but don't stint on affection and praise.

🐾 After you've charged the clicker, don't use it to get your dog's attention or to distract your dog from something, as this will be ultimately confusing. Only use the clicker to reinforce positive behavior.

🐾 Don't always train in the same place. Begin each new trick in an environment that's free of distractions. As your dog gets the hang of things, change locations and environments so that the trick is not dependent on being in the same place and circumstances.

🐾 Record your training sessions. Looking over them can help you spot a distraction in the environment, reveal that you're clicking too early or too late, or help you understand what's happening from your dog's viewpoint. Plus your dog might become a YouTube sensation!

Shake HANDS

Greetings, sir. I am pleased to meet your acquaintance.

*Y*our dog is almost always happy to see you, but teaching your dog to shake hands can bring a more formal air to the proceedings. When your dog is in a sitting position, stoop down in front of him. Say "Shake" and begin to touch one of his front paws with your finger. Be patient and just touch. Don't prod.

When your dog lifts this paw from the ground, click, take it in your hand, and shake. Reward your dog. Practice a few times each day until your dog will lift his own paw and offer it when you say "Shake."

Hint: Another option is to hold your hand in front of your dog and encourage him to paw at it. When he lifts his paw, take it and say "Shake."

This human custom is somewhat strange, but I'll give it a try!

How to BEG

Can you resist this face? I don't think so!

Although this seems like a fairly straightforward trick, it can actually provide good exercise for your dog. The beg position will strengthen her thigh muscles and help build lower back strength. To begin, make sure your dog is in the basic "Sit" position. Hold a treat in front of her nose, not quite within reach of her mouth. As your dog begins to move her head forward to take the treat, raise it higher. At first she will just follow it by raising her head, but as you continue up, she will have to push up to sit only on her hind legs with her front paws in the air.

The first time through, click and treat as soon as she lifts her front paws off the floor. As you continue to practice, increase the wait time before offering the reward so she will get used to remaining in the position.

After teaching this trick, make sure that you don't let your dog train you rather than the other way around. She should beg only on your command. If she approaches the dinner table while you and your family are eating a meal, do not mistake this for the behavior you want to teach. Don't give her food from the table—it will only reinforce her begging at mealtimes. Remember that you are the one to initiate the tricks, not your dog.

Hint: Some dogs may not have as much natural balance to be able to perform this trick easily. Be patient. Although they may take more time to learn, they'll catch on to the trick in the end.

Pleeeeeease? Pretty please?

How to JUMP

Look, up in the sky. It's a bird, it's a plane, it's me!

If your dog has a lot of energy, tap that enthusiasm by teaching him how to jump up. It's great exercise for both of you!

When your dog is in a fun and playful mood, hold a favorite treat high over his head and use the "Jump" command to encourage him to leap for it. If you need to, jump along with your pet once or twice to show him how it's done. If he jumps up even a little bit, click and treat.

Continue training every day, holding a treat over your dog's head and encouraging him to leap for it with the "Jump" command. Be enthusiastic and offer a lot of praise and affection. Pretty soon he'll get the idea and leap as high as he can.

Bet you can't jump higher than me!

Once he has mastered the trick, gradually reduce your own jumping until you're standing still while your dog leaps for the treat. From there, slowly eliminate the food reward until your dog jumps on command.

This trick works best with dogs that are naturally active, such as Jack Russell terriers. If your pet isn't particularly energetic, it may take more time and effort to instill the basics. But don't give up: Success comes with patience and perseverance.

Hint: Your dog will feel more comfortable performing this trick on grass because it provides better traction and a softer landing. Avoid training on slippery surfaces such as a waxed floor.

Jump over a Bar

Dogs love to jump as they play, so teaching your pet to leap over a bar on command should be easier than you might imagine.

Purchase a jump bar at your local pet store, or make your own using a broom or yardstick extended between two chairs. If your dog is small, you can prop the bar between two short stacks of books.

Set the bar relatively low to start, 12 to 18 inches off the floor for large dogs and about 6 inches for small breeds. With your pet on a leash, jump over the bar with her while giving the "Jump" command. Treat and praise her. Repeat three or four more times or until she shows signs of losing interest. Practice every day.

Once your dog is able to clear the bar with ease, gradually raise it higher until she must leap over it. Always praise your pet and reward her when she is successful. Pretty soon, she will make the jump on command while you are across the room. Occasionally reward her with a treat to maintain interest.

Hint: If your dog initially appears fearful of the bar, place it on the ground and let her walk over it several times with you standing beside her. Once she feels more comfortable, you can elevate the bar. If your dog accidentally runs into the bar during a jump, don't make a big deal out of it. Your calm attitude will help her quickly forget this negative experience. 🐾

Do I get a better treat if I jump higher?

Jump through a Hoop

Jumping through a hoop is a classic dog trick, and one of the easiest things to teach your pet. Best of all, it's appropriate for dogs of any age or size.

Begin by purchasing a hula hoop or similar toy if you don't already have one. (If the hoop comes with beads inside, remove them; the noise can be frightening to dogs.) Hold the hoop vertically on the floor with one hand, then give the command "Hoop" and lure your dog through the hoop. Click and treat. If your dog continually tries to go around the hoop instead of through it, position the hoop in a doorway to block his way.

Repeat this a few times until your dog easily walks through the hoop on command. Once he's comfortable, raise the hoop a few inches of the ground and repeat. Click and treat. Over the course of a few days, gradually raise the hoop higher and higher until your dog must jump to get through it.

Practice until your pet enthusiastically leaps through the hoop on your command.

If your dog trips while going through the hoop, release it immediately to avoid injury. Continue training as if nothing happened; if you react negatively to such an incident, your pet may pick up on your emotions and become afraid of the hoop.

Hint: Make this trick more exciting by decorating the hoop with colored ribbons and other dazzlers. Make sure they don't distract your dog or get in his way.

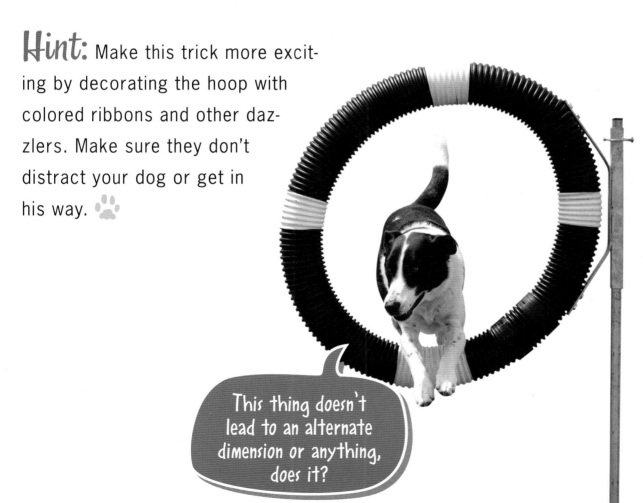

This thing doesn't lead to an alternate dimension or anything, does it?

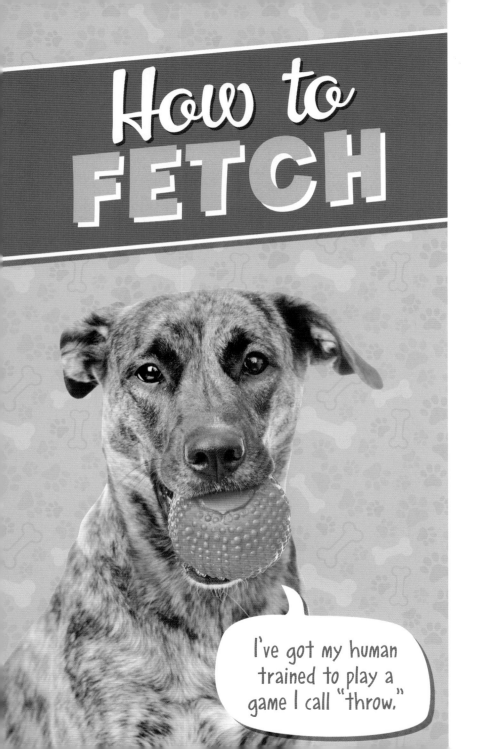

How to FETCH

I've got my human trained to play a game I call "throw."

Many dogs don't need to be taught to fetch something you toss—the instinct is in their genes. They may, however, need to learn how to bring it back and release it to you.

This trick uses two rubber balls to get things started. Hold one ball where it can get your dog's attention. Once your dog is interested, toss the ball a few feet away and say, "Fetch." If your dog gets the ball but doesn't bring it back, use the Come command. However, even if she returns, she may not want to give you the ball, which is where the second ball comes in.

Present the second ball to her, maybe tossing it from hand to hand or tossing it up and down in one hand—whatever you can do to make it appealing to her. When she drops the first ball and allows you to pick it up, click and treat, and toss the second ball for her to retrieve.

My human just keeps dropping the ball—she's lucky she's got me to pick it up each time!

Hint: Different breeds have different levels of interest in fetching. Although you need to repeat the trick and practice, make sure that you don't practice so long that your dog gets bored by the activity.

Fetch a Basket

If your dog is a natural "fetcher," teaching him to bring a basket to you on command should be a cinch. It's a fun trick and a great way to liven up a party or picnic.

I'm not quite sure how I became the cat's chauffeur...

Place a lightweight wicker basket in front of your pooch, and encourage him to pick it up by the handle. Most dogs will do this intuitively, but if your dog doesn't quite get it, hold the basket in front of him and gently encourage him to take the handle in his mouth. Click and reward your dog with praise.

Once your dog becomes accustomed to picking up the basket, add the "Bring it" command. Place the basket on the floor, take a few steps back, and say "Bring it." If your dog brings the basket to you successfully, reward him with affection. (Treats don't work with this particular trick because you don't want your pet to drop the basket.)

Gradually move farther away from your pet as you give the "Bring it" command, always rewarding him with affection when he does so. Once your dog becomes adept at picking up the basket and bringing it to you, place an object in the basket so he'll have something to carry. Continue the training. With enough practice, your pet will eagerly pick up the basket and bring it to you when ordered no matter where you are in the house or yard.

Fetch a Soda from the Refrigerator

Feeling lazy? It's pretty easy to teach your dog to bring you a soda (or a cold beer) from the refrigerator. You get a cool drink while simultaneously impressing your friends.

Start by teaching your pooch to open the refrigerator. Simply tie a long rag or dish towel to the door handle, and encourage your pet to pull on it, as if playing tug of war. When she successfully opens the door, click and treat. Next, teach her to close the refrigerator door by tapping on the front until she pushes it shut. Again, click and treat.

To teach your dog to bring you a drink, play fetch with an empty soda can until your pet is comfort

I'll fetch, you pour.

able carrying it in her mouth. Next, place the empty can on the lowest shelf in an open refrigerator and tell her to fetch it. When she takes the can in her mouth and brings it to you, click and treat. After a while, replace the empty can with one that hasn't been opened. Once your dog has mastered these basic steps, phase out the separate commands ("Open," "Fetch," "Close"), and simply say "Fetch me a soda."

Hint: If your dog won't take the empty can in her mouth because it is made of aluminum, place it in a foam insulator. This will also make the can easier for your pet to carry.

Man's best friend... and butler!

Play Mail CARRIER

Getting bills is much more fun when they're delivered by *someone* as adorable as me.

Dogs love to carry things around in their mouths, so it's relatively easy to teach your pet to become a letter carrier and deliver notes to others in your household.

Begin by having another person stand at the opposite end of a room that is free of distractions. (Your teaching partner should have some treats in his or her pocket.) Place a piece of paper in your dog's mouth, and give the command "Take mail." Point to the other person and say their name. The recipient should then encourage the dog to come to them.

When the dog arrives, the recipient should say the command "Give" and take the piece of paper from your pet's mouth. They should then reward the dog.

This is the kind of trick that is easily mastered with practice. Dogs, like humans, are adept at recognizing people by name if they hear the name often enough, so with a little effort you should be able to teach your pooch to deliver notes to everyone in your household.

Hint:
Folding the piece of paper will make it easier for your dog to pick it up if he drops it. Also, while you don't have to reward your pet with a treat every time he performs this trick, you should do so occasionally to reinforce the behavior. At the very least, your dog should receive some affection in the form of a pat on the head when he performs the trick successfully.

Will deliver for treats...

Catch a DISC

Good throw!

Flying discs are a favorite toy for many dogs because not only do they get to run and catch things, they also get to spend quality time with their owners. Another bonus: this is a fairly simple trick to learn.

Purchase an inexpensive plastic flying disc at a toy or pet store, and practice with it until you become adept at throwing it evenly. Next, introduce your pet to the disc and let him play with it. If necessary, encourage him by rolling the disc on its side.

When ready, take your pet to an open field, and lightly toss the disc in his direction while giving the command "Catch." Most dogs will instinctively try to catch the disc in their mouths. Click and praise your dog when he does this successfully, and encourage him to return the disc to you. Make the disc more desirable to your pet by hiding it behind your back between throws.

As your dog becomes more skilled at catching and returning the disc, gradually increase the distance between you and the dog so that he must run more and even leap to catch it.

Some dogs master this trick quite easily, but others have a little difficulty because it requires excellent coordination. Don't be discouraged if your pet doesn't pick it up right away; daily practice should make him a pro in no time.

Hint: This trick works best with medium and large-size dogs. Do not attempt it with small breeds or puppies because they could become injured as a result. 🐾

Fortunately, my human's aim has improved with practice.

Walk the PLANK

It's Bark Like a Pirate day.

$\mathcal{P}$irates are a popular Halloween costume, which is why it can be great fun to teach your dog to walk the plank.

For training purposes, begin with a board about 12 inches wide and 5 to 8 feet long. Once your pet has learned what to do, you can use a narrower board for a more exciting effect. Suspend the training board between two sturdy supports (low chairs or large buckets positioned upside down work well). Make sure the board is secure and doesn't move as your pet gets on and off.

First, teach your dog to jump up on the board by patting the board and giving the instruction "Up!" Click and treat when he climbs on the board or even touches it with his paw. Use praise and treats as positive reinforcements until he gets on the board upon command. Next, encourage your pet to walk the length of the plank by holding a treat in front of him and leading him along. Click and treat when he does this successfully. If he jumps off the board, gently correct him verbally, and place him back on. If necessary, gently use your hand or body to prevent him from jumping off.

Once your dog has mastered the basics of this trick, introduce narrower boards until he's able to walk along a board about four inches wide. Keep the board relatively low to the ground for your pet's safety.

Hint: This trick works best with small to medium-size dogs.

Let's take turns. You walk the plank. I'll take a nap.

Pirate Pooches

Turn over all your treats to me—or walk the plank!

Blackbeard had nothing on... Barkbeard.

PLAY Basketball

Michael Jordan's got nothing on me.

If your dog loves to carry a ball around in his mouth, you can easily teach him to play basketball. In fact, with enough practice, your pooch could become a canine LeBron James!

Purchase a child-size basketball set (available at any toy store), and lower it to the shortest setting so your pet can reach it without stretching. You'll also need

Nothing but net!

a small toy basketball for him to play with. Begin training by playing fetch with the ball. When your dog returns the ball to you, place a treat on the backboard and encourage him to drop the ball into the net with the "Dunk" command. The ball should fall out of his mouth as he reaches for the treat.

The goal is to make your dog understand that good things happen when he drops the ball into the hoop, so click and reward him even when he comes close. Once he gets the idea, reward him only when he correctly drops the ball through the hoop. When your dog is ready, stop rewarding him with treats and simply tap the backboard while giving the "Dunk" command. With sufficient practice, he'll learn to find the ball and drop it into the basket every time you say the word. Once your dog becomes adept at dunking, gradually raise the height of the basket to make the game more challenging.

Hint: If your dog is large enough, add some humor to this trick by dressing him in the jersey of your favorite basketball team. 🐾

He shoots! He scores! He...dribbles?

PLAY Soccer

I wonder if European breeds call this game "football"?

If basketball's not your dog's game, try out soccer! Begin by letting your dog examine and play with the ball. Each time she touches or even comes near to touching the ball with her nose, click and reward to reinforce the behavior. (Make sure to click exactly on the behavior—you don't want to click too late and reinforce the behavior of moving her nose away from the ball instead!) Over time, transition to clicking and rewarding when she nudges the ball with her nose in a way that moves or pushes it. It can be helpful to hold the ball loosely with your hands, keeping control of it so she doesn't get distracted by chasing after it if it moves.

When your dog has this down, put the ball right in front of the goal and let your dog push it in. Click and reward. Then work on increasing the distance between the ball and the goal. Reward your dog whenever she makes a goal!

Hint: If you don't have a goal, used a laundry basket turned on its side or have your dog nudge the soccer ball through the legs of a chair.

Aw, ref, that red flag just wasn't fair!

How to SPIN

This trick is both easy to learn and fun to watch! Hold a treat in front of your dog's nose, then slowly move it in a circle around your dog's body. Click as your dog turns around to follow the treat.

> I can make the world spin!

At first, encourage a quarter spin or a half spin. With practice, work up to a complete spin before you click and treat.

You can even teach your dog to know what direction to go by adding the verbal commands "left spin" or "right spin" as you train.

Hint: One step you can take to reinforce the behavior is to click and treat if your dog ever performs the action naturally.

I. Will. Catch. Up. To. My. Tail.

How to DANCE

Heeeey, Macarena!

If your dog knows how to sit up and beg, you're halfway to teaching him how to dance!

Begin with your dog in the begging position. Hold a treat just out of reach above his head. Encourage him to get the treat, and click and reward him when he stands up. Make sure you reward him only when his front paws are in the air so that he associates standing up with receiving a treat. If your dog tries to jump for the treat, however, pull back and do not reward him.

Once your dog has mastered standing up, click and reward only when he stands a little higher and you give the "Dance" command. Encourage him to stand for longer periods of time so that he gets used to balancing on his hind legs; reward him with a treat when he is successful. Don't be surprised if it takes your pet some time to master this, because it requires considerable conditioning. After all, standing on their hind legs is not something dogs ordinarily do.

When your dog has learned to stand for several seconds, start moving the treat around so that he takes small steps. This will make it look as if he is dancing. Click and reward him every time he does this successfully. Practice every day until your pet automatically rises up on his hind legs when you give the "Dance" command.

Hint: This trick works best with larger, more muscular dogs. Never attempt this trick with puppies, because their bones are still maturing and injury could result. 🐾

We're going to need to add a ballroom to my doghouse.

Play PIANO

We're not saying your dog will beat Mozart's mastery—but she can easily learn this fun party trick! Begin by encouraging your dog's curiosity about the piano—click and treat when she approaches or touches it. Over time, transition to clicking and rewarding when your dog interacts with the keyboard specifically, and then only when she uses her paws. Then click and reward only when a key is depressed and a note plays. Then build the behavior so that your

I'll play, but don't make me practice scales.

dog needs to touch the piano several times before being rewarded. As your dog gets the hang of it, add the verbal cue to "Play piano."

Hint: A sturdy toy piano or electronic keyboard works well for this trick. 🐾

I'm a musical genius!

How to SING

Depending on your dog, you may be able to shape this behavior from an existing behavior. If your dog has a particular bark or howl that sounds like "singing," click and treat whenever he uses it. Once your dog has associated singing with treats, add the verbal cue "Sing" to trigger the behavior. Do be careful with this, though—make sure that whatever bark or howl you reinforce is one you won't get tired of hearing!

I love singing along with my human!

This is the song that will get me into top 40.

If your dog doesn't bark or howl too often, you can try certain things to trigger the behavior—singing yourself, playing a song or a musical instrument, or even "howling" yourself.

Turn Off the LIGHTS

Look at me, helping save the environment!

Teaching your dog to turn off the lights can be both useful and entertaining.

Begin by holding your pet's favorite treat against the wall a few inches above the light switch. (A traditional flip switch works best.) Click and reward your pet with the treat when he successfully scratches at the switch. Repeat as necessary, adding in the verbal cue "Lights."

Next, enhance this behavior by holding a treat in your hand above the switch and a few inches away from the wall.

Tap the switch with your free hand while repeating the order "Lights." Click and reward him when he rises upright and paws the wall two or three times.

Once your dog gets the idea, tap the light switch while giving the order "Lights," then lower your hands and let your pet paw the wall by himself. Reward him every time he successfully paws the switch and turns the lights off. Repeat this exercise until your dog has it figured out.

For the final step, stand across the room and give the order "Lights." Your dog should immediately rise up and paw at the switch as instructed. Reward him with affection and a treat every time he is successful. Before you know it, your dog will be turning the lights off on command.

Hint: Tall dogs are best for this trick, but small dogs can easily learn it, too. However, they may need a stool or chair to safely reach the light switch. 🐾

I can cast the room into darkness, muahaha.

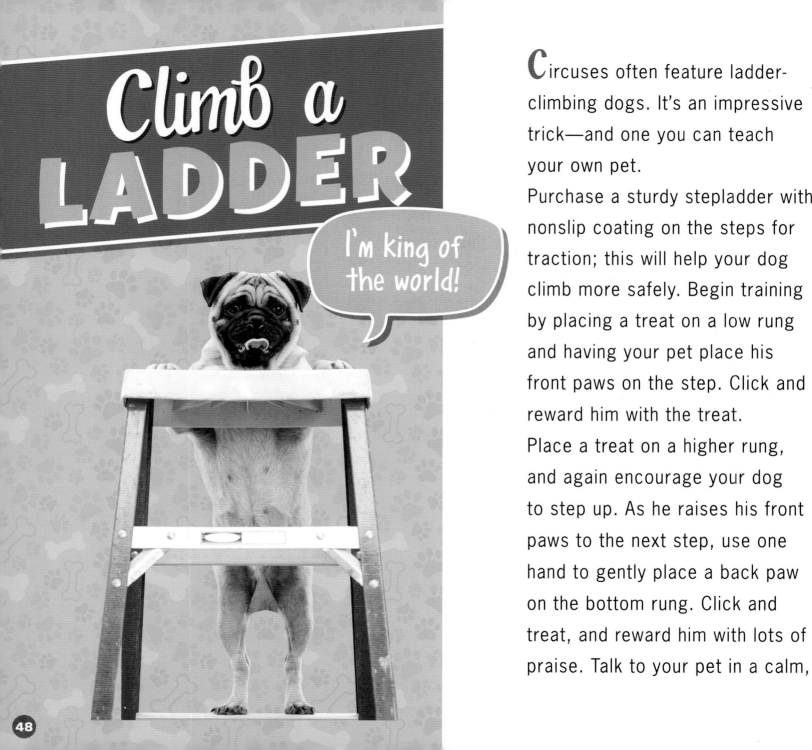

Climb a LADDER

I'm king of the world!

Circuses often feature ladder-climbing dogs. It's an impressive trick—and one you can teach your own pet.

Purchase a sturdy stepladder with nonslip coating on the steps for traction; this will help your dog climb more safely. Begin training by placing a treat on a low rung and having your pet place his front paws on the step. Click and reward him with the treat.

Place a treat on a higher rung, and again encourage your dog to step up. As he raises his front paws to the next step, use one hand to gently place a back paw on the bottom rung. Click and treat, and reward him with lots of praise. Talk to your pet in a calm, reassuring tone so he doesn't become frightened. Encourage your dog to climb higher still by placing a treat on the next rung. Reward him each time he is successful. When he finally climbs as high as he can, be effusive with praise and affection. You want his climb up the ladder to be fun and rewarding so he'll want to do it again. Over time, phase in the "climb" command as a verbal cue.

Practice this trick regularly until your dog becomes adept at climbing to the top of the ladder. Gradually reduce the number of treats necessary to engage the behavior until he climbs the ladder only on command.

Remember: You should always lift your dog off the ladder and set him down on the ground. Never allow him to jump off on his own.

Hint: If your dog panics while on the ladder, let him calm down before continuing with training. Never use force. 🐾

Look how high I am!

Balance Treat ON NOSE

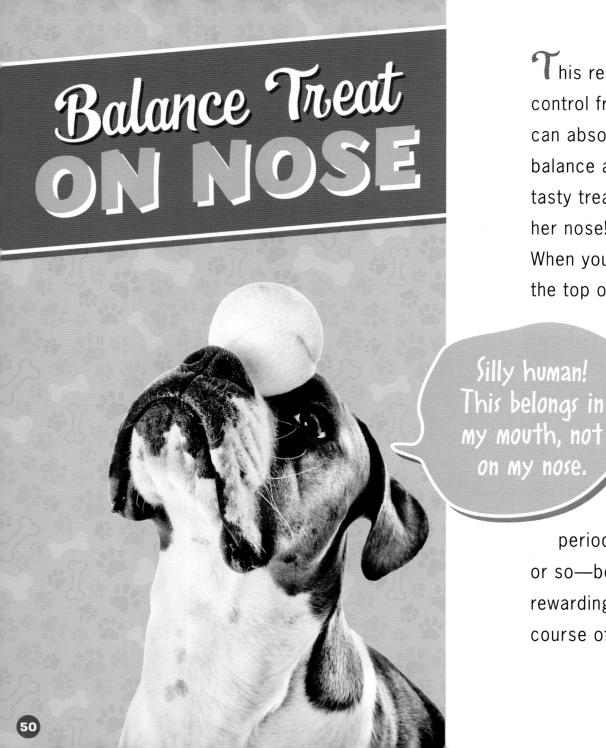

Silly human! This belongs in my mouth, not on my nose.

This requires a bit of impulse control from your dog, but you can absolutely train your dog to balance a ball, a toy, or even a tasty treat on the very end of her nose!

When your dog is sitting, touch the top of her muzzle gently. Click and reward her for sitting still. When she is comfortable with this, start placing the object gently on her nose for a very short period of time—just a second or so—before removing it and rewarding her. Build up over the course of several sessions to leaving the object for longer periods of time and removing your hand before clicking and rewarding.

Hint: First make sure that the object can be balanced—try balancing the object on a single finger first to make sure it's not lopsided or too heavy. 🐾

I do get to eat this at some point, right?

HOW TO Skateboard

You only wish you could be as cool as me.

It can take a little while to build this trick, and some dogs just won't have any interest or enjoyment. If your pooch does show an interest, though, this trick is very fun to watch!

Start by familiarizing your dog with the skateboard, holding it steady and then showing how it moves. At the beginning, click and reward when he interacts with it at all, then only when he puts a paw or paws on it. Hold the board still so it won't slide out from underneath him.

Once your dog is comfortable with putting both paws on the board, move it forward slowly, clicking and rewarding. His first instinct may be to get down off the skateboard, so be sure to click and reward before he does so. When that step is familiar, encourage your dog to move onto the board fully. After he has mastered that step, begin moving the board forward gently.

Hint: Bulldogs are known for being quick learners of this trick. It may be difficult to find a skateboard large enough to accommodate bigger breeds. 🐾

Next up, I'm trying an Ollie.

Bring the LEASH

Any houseguests you have will surely be impressed by this cute—and helpful—trick.
To begin, fold up the leash and place it near your dog. Encourage your dog to take the leash in her mouth, and click and

Walkies!

treat when she does. Add in the verbal cue of "get your leash." Once she has the verbal cue down, place the leash near the door, in a location where your dog can easily access it. From increasing distances, have your dog fetch the leash and bring it to you.

Build the next part of the sequence by encouraging her to drop the leash in your hands, clicking and treating when she does so. Take your dog outside for a walk as a special treat!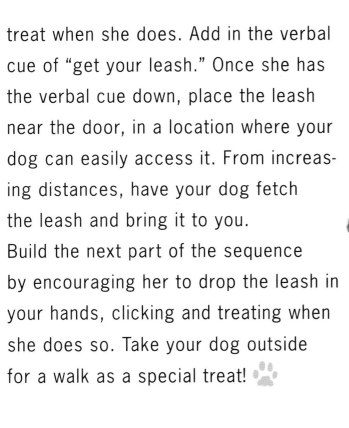

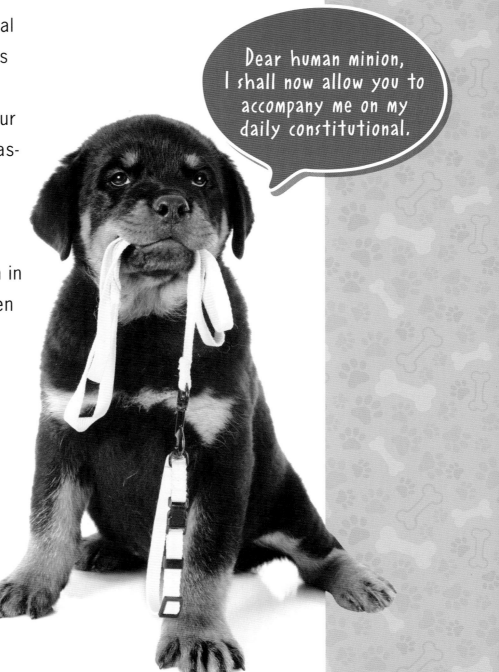

Dear human minion, I shall now allow you to accompany me on my daily constitutional.

Do Simple MATH

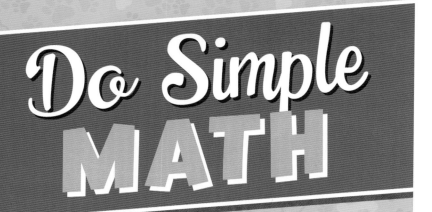

1 treat + 1 treat = 2 treats for me!

While this challenging trick takes a fair amount of time to teach, it will astonish your friends! When your dog has mastered this trick, you'll be able to have them pose a simple math problem to your dog and get a barked response.

Will your dog actually learn to count? Not exactly—although there is some evidence that dogs can recognize numbers up to about three or five. What you do in this trick is teach your dog to bark on cue, and to stop barking at a subtle signal. So technically you'll be doing any math problems…and you'll have to solve them correctly if you want your dog to look like a canine calculator!

Start with your dog sitting still and paying attention to you. Add a hand cue such as raising or lowering your hand. Click and treat when he barks. After several barks, lower your hand; click and treat only when he stops barking. Practice until your dog understands that a raised hand indicates that he start "speaking" and a lowered hand means he stops. Then practice making the hand cue more subtle over time, so that you don't give away the game to your guests! 🐾

How to READ

See Spot run.
Run, Spot,
run!

Teaching your dog to read is a matter of adding a visual cue to basic tricks she already knows. Use the cue cards enclosed in this kit, or create your own for other neat tricks in your dog's repertoire! Make sure the cue cards are visually distinct from each other.

Give your dog the command, such as "Sit." Hold up the "Sit" cue card as you do so. Click and reward your dog when she responds. Over time, you can

phase out the verbal command. After your dog has a handle on this, begin to hold up other cue cards during a training session—only click and treat when your dog responds to the "Sit" cue card.

Once she has a cue card mastered, introduce other cue cards and their associated commands. You'll be amazed at how quickly your dog will build up a "vocabulary" of commands! 🐾

Book Recommendations

The Catcher in the Rye is so profound, man. It speaks to me.

Allen Ginsberg's poem "Howl" just blew my mind!

When I'm in the mood for something historical, I pick up the ancient epic *Beowulf*— or as I call it, Be-a-Wolf.

How to BOW

It is now time for you to applaud.

Once your dog has done a series of tricks, it only makes sense for him to bow!

One method you can use to teach this trick is to reinforce a dog's natural behavior. Many dogs seem to "bow" as they stretch. Click and reward the behavior when it happens, gradually adding in a verbal command such as "take a bow." Over time, the dog will associate the verbal cue to "take a bow" with receiving a treat and will do it on command.

You can also encourage the behavior by teaching it, though. In this case it is helpful to use a long, thin stick of some sort. There are target sticks available to train your dog. Shape the behavior you would like to see, first by encouraging your dog to examine the stick and rewarding him for it, then by gradually lowering the target stick until your dog bends its elbows and lowers to the ground. Add the phrase "take a bow" in to describe the behavior. Practice the trick until your dog no longer needs the target stick but relies on the verbal cue phrase instead. 🐾

I'll be happy to do an encore!